BOX SET

- **FACTS ABOUT THE POISON DART FROGS**
- **FACTS ABOUT THE THREE TOED SLOTH**
- **FACTS ABOUT THE RED PANDA**
- **FACTS ABOUT THE SEAHORSE**
- **FACTS ABOUT THE PLATYPUS**
- **FACTS ABOUT THE REINDEER**
- **FACTS ABOUT THE PANTHER**
- **FACTS ABOUT THE SIBERIAN HUSKY**

LisaStrattin.com/BookBundle

Facts for Kids Picture Books by Lisa Strattin

Little Blue Penguin, Vol 92

Chipmunk, Vol 5

Frilled Lizard, Vol 39

Blue and Gold Macaw, Vol 13

Poison Dart Frogs, Vol 50

Blue Tarantula, Vol 115

African Elephants, Vol 8

Amur Leopard, Vol 89

Sabre Tooth Tiger, Vol 167

Baboon, Vol 174

Sign Up for New Release Emails Here

LisaStrattin.com/subscribe-here

Contents

INTRODUCTION

Hammerhead Sharks are named because of their flat shaped heads. They are large carnivorous fish that prey on large fish and occasionally will hunt small water mammals.

CHARACTERISTICS

There are 9 different species of Hammerhead Shark worldwide, ranging from 3ft to 20ft in length! They are not commonly known to attack humans, but can be aggressive if a person comes into contact with one.

The flat shaped head of the Hammerhead Shark is thought to allow the shark to locate prey easily, because this shape increases their sensitivity to sonar activity. They are thought to use sonar waves detection in a similar way to their other senses, so it's like the shark has a sixth sense!

Like many other species of shark, they are a solitary hunter during the night, but during the daytime they are known to form schools of up to 100 individuals. They are usually seen in larger groups during the summer months when they are migrating together in search of cooler waters.

APPEARANCE

The shape of the head of the Hammerhead Shark is made up of two projections on either side of the face, which gives their head the shape resembling a hammer.

The eyes and nostrils of the shark are found at the ends of the hammer giving the shark a better view and smell of the surrounding water.

TEMPERAMENT

The Great Hammerhead Shark is the largest species of hammerhead and one of their few species that is potentially dangerous to humans. This is because of the size of the Giant Hammerhead and also because they are known to be very aggressive.

Other species of these sharks tend to pose little or no threat to humans as they are generally much smaller and slightly calmer in nature.

LIFE SPAN

Hammerhead Sharks live for about 20 to 25 years on average.

SIZE

These adult Hammerhead Sharks are usually between 11 to 20 feet long and weigh between 500 to 1,000 pounds!

HABITAT

Hammerhead Sharks are found in the warmer waters of oceans all over the world, but most often live in coastal waters, and along continental shelves. The shallow waters allow them to hunt prey easier.

DIET

The Hammerhead Shark prefers to feast on fish, squid and octopus.

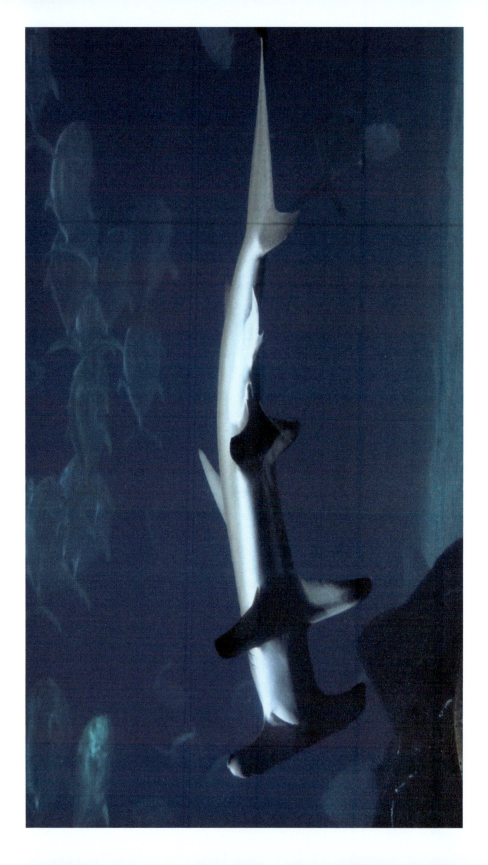

ENEMIES

There are some marine animals that like to hunt the Hammerhead Shark. These predators include: the Tiger Shark, the Great White Shark and Killer Whales.

SUITABILITY AS PETS

Well, of course you cannot have a Hammerhead Shark as a pet. If you want to see them, there are aquariums and zoos that have them in appropriate habitats. If you have a local zoo, you might be able to see them there.

COLOR ME

COLOR ME

COLOR ME

COLOR ME

COLOR ME

COLOR ME

COLOR ME

COLOR ME

Please leave me a review here:

LisaStrattin.com/Review-Vol-292

For more Kindle Downloads Visit Lisa Strattin Author Page on Amazon Author Central

amazon.com/author/lisastrattin

To see upcoming titles, visit my website at LisaStrattin.com– most books available on Kindle!

LisaStrattin.com

FREE BOOK

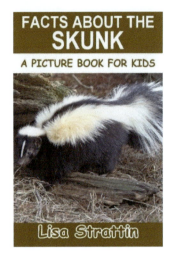

Printed in Great Britain
by Amazon

82304573R00025